HISTORY'S MOST INFLUENTIAL INVENTORS

FROM THE Early 1900s TO THE Mid-1900s

Henry Ford to Walt Disney

EDITED BY ROBERT CURLEY

Britannica® Educational Publishing

IN ASSOCIATION WITH

ROSEN EDUCATIONAL SERVICES

Published in 2025 by Britannica Educational Publishing
(a trademark of Encyclopædia Britannica, Inc.)
in association with Rosen Educational Services, LLC
2544 Clinton Street, Buffalo, NY 14224.

Distributed exclusively by Rosen Educational Services.
For a listing of additional Britannica Educational Publishing titles, call toll free (800) 237-9932.

First Edition

Britannica Educational Publishing
Michael I. Levy: Executive Editor
Marilyn L. Barton: Senior Coordinator, Production Control
Steven Bosco: Director, Editorial Technologies
Lisa S. Braucher: Senior Producer and Data Editor
Yvette Charboneau: Senior Copy Editor
Kathy Nakamura: Manager, Media Acquisition
Robert Curley: Manager, Science and Technology

Editor: Greg Roza
Book design: Michael Flynn

Photo credits: Cover https://commons.wikimedia.org/wiki/File:Henry-ford-american-industrialist-cars-made-in-usa-mass-production-detroit-freemasons-grand-lodge-of-new-york.jpg; pp. 6, 30 courtesy of the Library of Congress; p. 16 https://commons.wikimedia.org/wiki/File:Gliding_flight,_Wright_Glider,_Kitty_Hawk,_NC._1902.10459_A.S..jpg.

Cataloging-in-Publication Data

Names: Curley, Robert, 1955-.
Title: From the early 1900s to the mid-1900s: Henry Ford to Walt Disney / edited by Robert Curley.
Description: New York : Britannica Educational Publishing, in Association with Rosen Educational Services, 2025. | Series: History's most influential inventors | Includes glossary and index.
Identifiers: ISBN 9781641900966 (library bound) | ISBN 9781641900959 (pbk) | ISBN 9781641900973 (ebook)
Subjects: LCSH: Inventors--Biography. | Inventions--History.
Classification: LCC T39.F766 2025 | DDC 609.2'2--dc23

Manufactured in the United States of America

CPSIA Compliance Information: Batch #CSBRIT25. For further information contact Rosen Publishing at 1-800-237-9932.

CONTENTS

Introduction

"I invented nothing new. I simply assembled the discoveries of other men behind whom were centuries of work. Had I worked fifty or ten or even five years before, I would have failed. So it is with every new thing."
—Henry Ford (1863–1947)

Life has been transformed over the years through the efforts of the men and women who had the brilliance, diligence, and creativity to come up with new and better ways of doing things. This book focuses on the inventions of people who lived from the early 1900s to the mid-1900s. These inventors clearly improved life by keeping people healthier, helping them to communicate and work more efficiently, and allowing them to travel farther. As detailed throughout these pages, their inventions spawned many more inventions, speeding up the pace of progress even further.

What ultimately fueled the spark of discovery and led inventors to their "eureka" moment was unique to each person. Dr. Robert H. Goddard, who pioneered the first rocket-powered spacecraft, became fascinated with the idea of space flight after reading H.G. Wells's science fiction novel *The War of the Worlds*. Decades before Henry Ford introduced the Model T automobile and designed the moving assembly line, he became fascinated with the inner workings of clocks and watches.

Despite the hard work that was often required to produce an invention, money was not always the impetus for the inventors in this book. Yet some inventors saw great success during their lifetimes. When Ford died in 1947, his estimated net worth was around $600 million.

Money was just one of the benefits awarded to those

who came up with a successful invention. Inventors also earned fame, recognition, and a place in history. Some received what is thought to be the highest honor—the Nobel Prize. In 1909, Guglielmo Marconi received the Nobel Prize in Physics for developing the first practical radio.

In 1948, Paul Hermann Müller received a Nobel Prize for discovering the toxic effects on insects of the chemical compound known as DDT, a pesticide that efficiently wiped out the insects that carry deadly diseases such as malaria, yellow fever, and typhus. DDT was initially hailed as a "miracle" pesticide. Yet by the early 1970s it had been banned from public use in the United States. Health officials had discovered that while DDT was killing insects, it was also accumulating in other wildlife, notably falcons and eagles, and dangerously lowering their reproduction rate.

This book recognizes not only the inventors whose work changed the course of human life, but also those whose ideas paved the way for future generations of inventors. Often inventors were inspired by one another. For example, Orville and Wilbur Wright became interested in aviation after reading about German aviation engineer Otto Lilienthal's experiments with gliders. In turn, the Wright Brothers' famous 1903 flight at Kitty Hawk, North Carolina, inspired a teenaged Russian boy named Igor Sikorsky to later invent the world's first single-rotor helicopter.

So many inventors have made important contributions in this time period that to mention them all here would far exceed the space limitations of this book. The figures who have been included are among the greatest and most prolific inventors of all time. They were selected because their inventions have altered the course of people's lives and have left an indelible stamp on human history.

The 1909 Model T. Courtesy of the Ford Motor Company.

HENRY FORD

(b. July 30, 1863, Wayne county, Mich., U.S.—d. April 7, 1947, Dearborn, Mich.)

Henry Ford was an American industrialist who revolutionized factory production with his assembly line methods, which he applied in particular to his car for the common man, the Model T.

Ford spent most of his life making headlines, good, bad, but never indifferent. Celebrated as both a technological genius and a folk hero, Ford was the creative force behind an industry of unprecedented size and wealth that in only a few decades permanently changed the economic and social character of the United States. When young Ford left his father's farm in 1879 for Detroit, only two out of eight Americans lived in cities; when he died at age 83, the proportion was five out of eight. Once Ford realized the tremendous part he and his Model T automobile had played in bringing about this change, he wanted nothing more than to reverse it, or at least to recapture the rural values of his boyhood. Henry Ford, then, is an apt symbol of the transition from an agricultural to an industrial America.

EARLY LIFE

Henry Ford was one of eight children of William and Mary Ford. He was born on the family farm near Dearborn, Michigan, then a town eight miles west of Detroit. Abraham Lincoln was president of the 24 states of the Union, and Jefferson Davis was president of the 11 states of the Confederacy. Ford attended a one-room school for eight years when he was not helping his father with the harvest. At age 16 he walked to Detroit to find work in its machine shops. After three years, during which he came in contact with the internal-combustion engine for the first time, he returned to the farm, where he worked part-time for the Westinghouse Engine Company and in spare moments tinkered in a little machine shop he set up. Eventually he built a small "farm locomotive," a tractor that used an old mowing machine for its chassis and a homemade steam engine for power.

GOING INTO BUSINESS

Ford moved back to Detroit nine years later as a married man. His wife, Clara Bryant, had grown up on a farm not far from Ford's. They were married in 1888, and on November 6, 1893, she gave birth to their only child, Edsel Bryant. A month later Ford was made chief engineer at the main Detroit Edison Company plant with responsibility for maintaining electric service in the city 24 hours a day. Because he was on call at all times, he had no regular hours and could experiment to his heart's content. He had determined several years before to build a gasoline-powered vehicle, and his first working gasoline engine was completed at the end of 1893. By 1896 he had completed his first horseless carriage, the "Quadricycle," so called because the chassis of the four-horsepower vehicle was a buggy frame mounted on four bicycle wheels. Unlike many other automotive inventors, including Charles Edgar and J. Frank Duryea, Elwood Haynes, Hiram Percy Maxim, and his Detroit acquaintance Charles Brady King, all of whom had built self-powered vehicles before Ford but who held onto their creations, Ford sold his to finance work on a second vehicle, and a third, and so on.

During the next seven years he had various backers, some of whom, in 1899, formed the Detroit Automobile Company (later the Henry Ford Company), but all eventually abandoned him in exasperation because they wanted a passenger car to put on the market while Ford insisted always on improving whatever model he was working on, saying that it was not ready yet for customers. He built several racing cars during these years, including the "999" racer driven by Barney Oldfield, and set several new speed records. In 1902 he left the Henry Ford Company, which subsequently reorganized as the Cadillac Motor Car Company. Finally, in 1903, Ford was ready to market an automobile. The Ford Motor Company was incorporated, this time with a mere $28,000 in cash put up by ordinary citizens, for Ford had, in his previous dealings with backers, antagonized the wealthiest men in Detroit.

The company was a success from the beginning, but just five weeks after its incorporation the Association of Licensed Automobile Manufacturers threatened to put it out of business because Ford was not a licensed manufacturer. He had been denied a license by this group, which aimed at reserving for its members the profits of what was fast becoming a major industry. The basis of their power was control of a patent granted in 1895 to George Baldwin Selden, a patent lawyer of Rochester, New York. The association claimed that the patent applied to all gasoline-powered automobiles. Along with many rural Midwesterners of his generation, Ford hated industrial combinations and Eastern financial power. Moreover, Ford thought the Selden patent was preposterous. All invention was a matter of evolution, he said, yet Selden claimed genesis. He was glad to fight, even though the fight pitted the puny Ford Motor Company against an industry worth millions of dollars. The gathering of evidence and actual court hearings took six years. Ford lost the original case in 1909; he appealed and won the case in 1911. His victory had wide implications for the industry, and the fight made Ford a popular hero.

THE MODEL T AND THE ASSEMBLY LINE

"I will build a motor car for the great multitude," Ford proclaimed in announcing the birth of the Model T in October 1908. In the 19 years of the Model T's existence, he sold 15,500,000 of the cars in the United States, almost 1,000,000 more in Canada, and 250,000 in Great Britain, a production total amounting to half the auto output of the world. The motor age arrived owing mostly to Ford's vision of the car as the ordinary man's utility rather than as the rich man's luxury. Once only the rich had traveled freely around the country; now millions could go wherever they pleased. The Model T was the chief instrument of one of the greatest and most rapid changes in the lives of the common people in history, and it effected this change in less than two decades. Farmers were no longer isolated on remote farms. The horse disappeared so rapidly that the transfer of acreage from hay to other crops caused an agricultural revolution. The automobile became the main prop of the American economy and a stimulant to urbanization—cities spread outward, creating suburbs and housing developments—and to the building of the finest highway system in the world.

The remarkable birthrate of Model T's was made possible by the most advanced production technology yet conceived. After much experimentation by Ford and his engineers, the system that had evolved by 1913–14 in Ford's new plant in Highland Park, Michigan, was able to deliver parts, subassemblies, and assemblies (themselves built on subsidiary assembly lines) with precise timing to a constantly moving main assembly line, where a complete chassis was turned out every 93 minutes, an enormous improvement over the 728 minutes formerly required. The minute subdivision of labor and the coordination of a multitude of operations produced huge gains in productivity.

In 1914 the Ford Motor Company announced that it would henceforth pay eligible workers a minimum wage of $5 a day (compared to an average of $2.34 for the industry) and would reduce the workday from nine hours to eight, thereby converting the factory to a three-shift day. Overnight Ford became a worldwide celebrity. People either praised him as a great humanitarian or excoriated him as a mad socialist. Ford said humanitarianism had nothing to do with it. Previously profit had been based on paying wages as low as workers would take and pricing cars as high as the traffic would bear. Ford, on the other hand, stressed low pricing (the Model T cost $950 in 1908 and $290 in 1927) in order to capture the widest possible market and then met the price by volume and efficiency. Ford's success in making the automobile a basic necessity turned out to be but a prelude to a more widespread revolution. The development of mass-production techniques, which enabled the company eventually to turn out a Model T every 24 seconds; the frequent reductions in the price of the car made possible by economies of scale; and the payment of a living wage that raised workers above subsistence and made them potential customers for, among other things, automobiles—these innovations changed the very structure of society.

WILBUR AND ORVILLE WRIGHT

respectively, (b. April 16, 1867, near Millville, Ind., U.S.—d. May 30, 1912, Dayton, Ohio), ; (b. Aug. 19, 1871, Dayton—d. Jan. 30, 1948, Dayton)

The Wright brothers, Wilbur and Orville, were American inventors and aviation pioneers who achieved the first powered, sustained, and controlled airplane flight (1903) and built and flew the first fully practical airplane (1905).

Early Family Life

Wilbur and Orville were the sons of Milton Wright, an ordained minister of the Church of the United Brethren in Christ, and Susan Catherine Koerner Wright, whom Milton had met while he was training for the ministry and while Susan was a student at a United Brethren college in Hartsville, Ind. Two boys, Reuchlin (1861–1920) and Lorin (1862–1939), were born to the couple before Wilbur was born on a farm near Millville, Indiana. The young family then moved to Dayton, Ohio, so that Milton could take up duties as the editor of a church newspaper. In that city a pair of twins, Otis and Ida, were born and died in 1870. Orville arrived a year later, followed by Katharine (1874–1929).

Elected a bishop of the church in 1877, Milton spent long periods of time away from home visiting the Brethren congregations for which he was responsible. The family moved often: to Cedar Rapids, Iowa, in 1878; to a farm near Richmond, Indiana, in 1881; and back to Dayton in 1884. The Wright children were educated in public schools and grew up, as Orville later explained, in a home where "there was always much encouragement to children to pursue intellectual interests; to investigate whatever aroused curiosity." In a less-nourishing environment, Orville believed, "our curiosity might have been nipped long before it could have borne fruit."

These were not tranquil years for Bishop Wright. As the leader of a conservative faction opposed to modernization in the church, he was involved in a 20-year struggle that led to a national schism in 1889 and was followed by multiple lawsuits for possession of church property. Even as these decades of crisis were approaching a conclusion, an entirely new conflict developed, this time within the small schismatic branch that Bishop Wright had led away from the original church. The resulting church disciplinary hearings and civil court cases continued up to the time of the bishop's retirement in 1905.

Bishop Wright exercised an extraordinary influence on the lives of his children. Wilbur and Orville, like their father, were independent thinkers with a deep confidence in their own talents, an unshakable faith in the soundness of their judgment, and a determination to persevere in the face of disappointment and adversity. Those qualities, when combined with their unique technical gifts, help to explain the success of the Wright brothers as inventors. At the same time, the bishop's rigid adherence to principle and disinclination to negotiate disputes may have had some influence on the manner in which the brothers, later in life, conducted the marketing of their invention.

Printers and Bicycle Makers

Wilbur and Orville were the only members of the Wright family who did not attend college or marry. Wilbur's plans to enter college came to an end when he was injured in a hockey accident in the winter of 1885–86. He spent the following three years recovering his health, reading extensively in his father's library, assisting the bishop with his legal and church problems, and caring for his invalid mother, who died of tuberculosis in 1889.

Following their mother's death, Orville, who had spent several summers learning the printing trade, persuaded Wilbur to join him in establishing a print shop. In addition to normal printing services, the brothers edited and published two short-lived local newspapers, and they also developed a local reputation for the quality of the presses that they designed, built, and sold to other printers. These printing presses were one of the first indications of the Wright brothers' extraordinary technical ability and their unique approach to the solution of problems in mechanical design.

In 1892 the brothers opened a bicycle sales and repair shop, and they began to build bicycles on a small scale in 1896. They developed their own self-oiling bicycle wheel hub and installed a number of light machine tools in the shop. Profits from the print shop and the bicycle operation eventually were to fund the Wright brothers' aeronautical experiments from 1899 to 1905. In addition, the experience of designing and building lightweight, precision machines of wood, wire, and metal tubing was ideal preparation for the construction of flying machines.

In later years the Wrights dated their fascination with flight to a small helicopter toy that their father had brought home from his travels when the family was living in Iowa. A decade later, they had read accounts of the work of the German glider pioneer Otto Lilienthal. But it was news reports of Lilienthal's death in a glider crash in August 1896 that marked the beginning of their serious interest in flight. By 1899 the brothers had exhausted the resources of the local library and had written to the Smithsonian Institution for suggestions as to further reading in aeronautics. The following year they wrote to introduce themselves to Octave Chanute, a leading civil engineer and an authority on aviation who would remain a confidant of the brothers during the critical years from 1900 to 1905.

Early Glider Experiments

The ability of the Wright brothers to analyze a mechanical problem and move toward a solution was apparent from the outset of their work in aeronautics. The brothers realized that a successful airplane would require wings to generate lift, a propulsion system to move it through the air, and a system to control the craft in flight. Lilienthal, they reasoned, had built wings capable of carrying him in flight, while the builders of self-propelled vehicles were developing lighter and more powerful internal-combustion engines. The final problem to be solved, they concluded, was that of control.

Most aeronautical experimenters up to that time had sought to develop flying machines incorporating a measure of inherent stability, so that the aircraft would tend to fly a straight and level course unless the pilot intervened to change altitude or direction. As experienced cyclists, the Wrights preferred to place complete control of their machine in the hands of the operator. Moreover, aware of the dangers of weight-shifting control (a means of controlling the aircraft by shifting the position of the pilot), the brothers were determined to control their machine through a precise manipulation of the center of pressure on the wings. After considering various mechanical schemes for obtaining such control, they decided to try to induce a helical twist across the wings in either direction. The resulting increase in lift on one side and decrease on the other would enable the pilot to raise or lower either wing tip at will.

Their first experiments with "wing warping," as the system would be called, were made with a small biplane kite flown in Dayton in the summer of 1899. Discovering that they could cause the kite to climb, dive, and bank to the right or left at will, the brothers began to design their first full-scale glider using Lilienthal's data to calculate the amount of wing surface area required to lift the estimated weight of the machine and pilot in a wind of given velocity.

Realizing that Dayton, with its relatively low winds and flat terrain, was not the ideal place to conduct aeronautical experiments, the Wrights requested of the U.S. Weather Bureau a list of more suitable areas. They selected Kitty Hawk, an isolated village on the Outer Banks of North Carolina, which offered high average winds, tall dunes from which to glide, and soft sand for landings.

Tested in October 1900, the first Wright glider was a biplane featuring 165 square feet (15 square meters) of wing area and a forward elevator for pitch control. The glider developed less lift than expected, however, and very few free flights were made with a pilot on board. The brothers flew the glider as a kite, gathering information on the performance of the machine that would be critically important in the design of future aircraft.

Eager to improve on the disappointing performance of their 1900 glider, the Wrights increased the wing area of their next machine to 290 square feet (26 square meters). Establishing their camp at the foot of the Kill Devil Hills, 4 miles (6.5 km) south of Kitty Hawk, the brothers completed 50 to 100 glides in July and August of 1901. As in 1900, Wilbur made all the glides, the best of which covered nearly 400 feet (120 m). The 1901 Wright aircraft was an improvement over its predecessor, but it still did not perform as well as their calculations had predicted. Moreover, the experience of 1901 suggested that the prob-

This 1902 photo depicts Wilbur Wright flying the glider biplane he designed with the help of his brother Orville.

lems of control were not fully resolved.

Discouraged, but determined to preserve a record of their aeronautical work to date, Wilbur accepted Chanute's invitation to address the prestigious Western Society of Engineers. Wilbur's talk was delivered in Chicago on September 18, 1901, and was published as "Some Aeronautical Experiments" in the journal of the society. It indicated the extent to which the Wright brothers, in spite of their disappointments, had already moved beyond other flying machine experimenters.

Solving the Problems of Lift and Control

Realizing that the failure of their gliders to match calculated performance was the result of errors in the experimental data published by their predecessors, the Wrights constructed a small wind tunnel with which to gather their own information on the behavior in an airstream of model wings of various shapes and sizes. The brilliance of the Wright brothers, their ability to visualize the behavior of a machine that had yet to be constructed, was seldom more apparent than in the design of their wind-tunnel balances, the instruments mounted inside the tunnel that actually measured the forces operating on the model wings. During the fall and early winter of 1901 the Wrights tested between 100 and 200 wing designs in their wind tunnel, gathering information on the relative efficiencies of various airfoils and determining the effect of different wing shapes, tip designs, and gap sizes between the two wings of a biplane.

With the results of the wind-tunnel tests in hand, the brothers began work on their third full-scale glider. They tested the machine at the Kill Devil Hills camp in September and October of 1902. It performed exactly as the design calculations predicted. For the first time, the brothers shared the flying duties, completing 700 to 1,000 flights, covering distances up to 622.5 feet (189.75 m), and remaining in the air for as long as 26 seconds. In addition to gaining significant experience in the air, the Wrights were able to complete their control system by adding a movable rudder linked to the wing-warping system.

Powered, Sustained Flight

With the major aerodynamic and control problems behind them, the brothers pressed forward with the design and construction of their first powered machine. They designed and built a four-cylinder internal-combustion engine with the assistance of Charles Taylor, a machinist whom they employed in the bicycle shop. Recognizing that propeller blades could be understood as rotary wings, the Wrights were able to design twin pusher propellers on the basis of their wind-tunnel data.

The brothers returned to their camp near the Kill Devil Hills in September 1903. They spent the next seven weeks assembling, testing, and repairing their powered machine and conducting new flight tests with the 1902 glider. Wilbur made the first attempt at powered flight on December 14, but he stalled the aircraft on takeoff and damaged the forward section of the machine. Three days were spent making repairs and waiting for the return of good weather. Then, at about 10:35 on the morning of December 17, 1903, Orville made the first successful flight, covering 120 feet (36 m) through the air in 12 seconds. Wilbur flew 175 feet (53 m) in 12 seconds on his first attempt, followed by Orville's second effort of 200 feet (60 m) in 15 seconds. During the fourth and final flight of the day, Wilbur flew 852 feet (259 m) over the sand in 59 seconds. The four flights were witnessed by five local citizens. For the first time in history, a heavier-than-air machine had demonstrated powered and sustained flight under the complete control of the pilot.

Determined to move from the marginal success of 1903 to a practical airplane, the Wrights in 1904 and 1905 built and flew two more aircraft from Huffman Prairie, a pasture near Dayton. They continued to improve the design of their machine during these years, gaining skill and confidence in the air. By October 1905 the brothers could remain aloft for up to 39 minutes at a time, performing circles and other maneuvers. Then, no longer able to hide the extent of their success from the press, and concerned that the essential features of their machine would be understood and copied by knowledgeable observers, the Wrights decided to cease flying and remain on the ground until their invention was protected by patents and they had negotiated a contract for its sale.

Making the Invention Public

The claim of the Wright brothers to have flown was widely doubted during the years 1906–07. During that period a handful of European and American pioneers struggled into the air in machines designed on the basis of an incomplete understanding of Wright technology. Meanwhile the brothers, confident that they retained a commanding lead over their rivals, continued to negotiate with financiers and government purchasing agents on two continents.

In February 1908 the Wrights signed a contract for the sale of an airplane to the U.S. Army. They would receive $25,000 for delivering a machine capable of flying for at least one hour with a pilot and passenger at an average speed of 40 miles (65 km) per hour. The following month, they signed a second agreement with a group of French investors interested in building and selling Wright machines under license.

With the new aircraft that they would fly in America and France ready for assembly, the Wright brothers returned to the Kill Devil Hills in May 1908, where they made 22 flights with their old 1905 machine, modified with upright seating and hand controls. On May 14, 1908, Wilbur carried aloft the first airplane passenger—the mechanic Charles Furnas.

Wilbur then sailed to France, where he captured the European imagination with his first public flight; this took place over the Hunaudières Race Course near Le Mans on August 8, 1908. During the months that followed, the elite of the continent traveled to watch Wilbur fly at Le Mans and Pau in France and at Centocelle near Rome.

Orville began the U.S. Army trials at Fort Myer, Virginia, with a flight on September 3, 1908. Fourteen days later a split propeller precipitated a crash that killed his passenger, Lt. Thomas E. Selfridge, and badly injured the pilot. During the course of his recovery, Orville and his sister Katharine visited Wilbur in Europe. Together, the brothers returned to Fort Myer to complete the Army trials in 1909. Having exceeded the required speed of 40 miles (65 km) per hour, the Wrights earned a bonus of $5,000 beyond the $25,000 contract price.

Following the successful Fort Myer trials, Orville traveled to Germany, where he flew at Berlin and Potsdam. Wilbur made several important flights as part of New York City's Hudson-Fulton Celebration, then went to College Park, Maryland, where he taught the first three U.S. Army officers to fly.

Going into Business

In November 1909 the Wright Company was

incorporated with Wilbur as president, Orville as one of two vice presidents, and a board of trustees that included some of the leaders of American business. The Wright Company established a factory in Dayton and a flying field and flight school at Huffman Prairie. Among the pilots trained at the facility was Henry H. "Hap" Arnold, who would rise to command of the U.S. Army Air Forces during World War II.

The brothers also formed the Wright Exhibition Company in March 1910, with A. Roy Knabenshue, an experienced balloon and airship pilot, as manager. Although the Wrights were not eager to enter what they regarded as a "mountebank business," they recognized that an exhibition team would generate steady revenues to supplement funds received from the sale of aircraft, flight instruction, and license fees. Orville began training pilots for the exhibition team at Montgomery, Alabama, and continued instruction at Huffman Prairie. The exhibition company made its first appearance at Indianapolis, Indiana, in June 1910 and remained in business until November 1911, by which time the deaths of several team members convinced the Wright brothers to discontinue operations.

After the summer of 1909, Wilbur focused his energies on business and legal activities. He took the lead in bringing a series of lawsuits against rival aircraft builders in the United States and Europe who the brothers believed had infringed upon their patent rights. In Germany, the Wright claims were disallowed on the basis of prior disclosure. Even in France and America, where the position of the Wright brothers was upheld in virtually every court judgment, the defendants were able to manipulate the legal process in such a manner as to avoid substantial payments. Moreover, the Wrights' spirited pursuit of their international patent rights significantly complicated their public image. Once inaccurately regarded as a pair of naive mechanical geniuses, they were now unfairly blamed for having retarded the advance of flight technology by bringing suit against other talented experimenters. The era of the lawsuits came to an effective end in 1917, when the Wright patents expired in France and the U.S. government created a patent pool in the interest of national defense.

Orville Carries on the Legacy

Exhausted by business and legal concerns and suffering from typhoid fever, Wilbur died in his bed early on the morning of May 30, 1912. Wilbur had drawn Orville into aeronautics and had taken the lead in business matters since 1905. Upon Wilbur's decease, Orville assumed leadership of the Wright Company, remaining with the firm until 1915, when he sold his interest in the company to a group of financiers. He won the 1913 Collier Trophy for his work on an automatic stabilizer for aircraft, and he worked as a consulting engineer during World War I, helping the Dayton-Wright Company plan for the production of foreign aircraft designs and assisting in the development of a pilotless aircraft bomb.

One of the most celebrated Americans of his time, Orville received honorary degrees and awards from universities and organizations across America and Europe. He remained active in aeronautics as a member of the National Advisory Committee for Aeronautics (1920–48) and as a leader of other organizations, notably the advisory board of the Daniel and Florence Guggenheim Fund for the Promotion of Aeronautics. Orville disliked public speaking, however, and enjoyed nothing more than spending time with friends and family in the privacy of his home and laboratory in Dayton or his vacation retreat on Georgian Bay, off of Lake Huron in Ontario, Canada. During the last four decades of his life he devoted considerable energy to defending the priority of the Wright brothers as the inventors of the airplane. A long-running feud with the leadership of the Smithsonian Institution was particularly noteworthy. During the years prior to World War I, Smithsonian officials claimed that the third secretary of the institution, S.P. Langley, had constructed a machine "capable" of flight prior to the Wrights' success of December 1903. Unable to obtain a retraction of this claim by 1928, Orville lent the restored 1903 airplane to the Science Museum in London and did not consent to bringing the machine to Washington, D.C., until after the Smithsonian offered an apology in 1942.

On January 27, 1948, Orville suffered a heart attack; he died three days later in a Dayton hospital. There is perhaps no better epitaph for both of the Wright brothers than the words crafted by a group of their friends to appear as a label identifying the 1903 Wright airplane on display at the Smithsonian: "By original scientific research, the Wright brothers discovered the principles of human flight. As inventors, builders and flyers, they further developed the aeroplane, taught man to fly, and opened the era of aviation."

LEE DE FOREST

(b. Aug. 26, 1873, Council Bluffs, Iowa, U.S.—d. June 30, 1961, Hollywood, Calif.)

Lee De Forest was an American inventor of the Audion vacuum tube, which made possible live radio broadcasting and became the key component of all radio, telephone, radar, television, and computer systems before the invention of the transistor in 1947. Although bitter over the financial exploitation of his inventions by others, he was widely honored as the "father of radio" and the "grandfather of television." He was supported strongly but unsuccessfully for the Nobel Prize for Physics.

Life

De Forest was the son of a Congregational minister. His father moved the family to Alabama and there assumed the presidency of the nearly bankrupt Talladega College for Negroes. Ostracized by citizens of the white community who resented his father's efforts to educate Blacks, Lee made his friends from among the Black children of the town and, together with his brother and sister, spent a happy although sternly disciplined childhood in this rural community.

As a child, he was fascinated with machinery and was often excited when hearing of the many technological advances during the late 19th century. By age 13 he was an enthusiastic inventor of mechanical gadgets, such as a miniature blast furnace and locomotive and a working silver-plating apparatus.

His father had planned for him a career in the clergy, but Lee insisted on science and, in 1893, enrolled at the Sheffield Scientific School of Yale University, one of the few institutions in the United States then offering a first-class scientific education. Frugal and hardworking, he supplemented his scholarship and the slim allowance provided by his parents by working at menial jobs during his college years, and, despite a not-too-distinguished undergraduate career, he went on to earn the Ph.D. in physics in 1899.

By this time he had become interested in electricity, particularly the study of electromagnetic-wave propagation, then being pioneered chiefly by the German Heinrich Rudolf Hertz and the Italian Guglielmo Marconi. De Forest's doctoral dissertation on the "Reflection of Hertzian Waves from the Ends of Parallel Wires" was possibly the first doctoral thesis in the United States on the subject that was later to become known as radio.

His first job was with the Western Electric Company in Chicago, where, beginning in the dynamo department, he worked his way up to the telephone section and then to the experimental laboratory. While working after hours on his own, he developed an electrolytic detector of Hertzian waves. The device was modestly successful, as was an alternating-current transmitter that he designed. In 1902 he and his financial backers founded the De Forest Wireless Telegraph Company. In order to dramatize the potential of this new medium of communication, he began, as early as 1902, to give public demonstrations of wireless telegraphy for businessmen, the press, and the military.

Invention of the Audion Tube

A poor businessman and a poorer judge of men, De Forest was defrauded twice by his own business partners. By 1906 his first company was insolvent, and he had been squeezed out of its operation. But in 1907 he patented a much more promising detector (developed in 1906), which he called the Audion; it was capable of more sensitive reception of wireless signals than were the electrolytic and Carborundum types then in use. It was a thermionic grid-triode vacuum tube—a three-element electronic "valve" similar to a two-element device patented by the Englishman Sir John Ambrose Fleming in 1905. In 1907 De Forest was able to broadcast experimentally both speech and music to the general public in the New York City area.

A second company, the De Forest Radio Telephone Company, began to collapse in 1909, again because of some of his partners. In the succeeding legal confusion, De Forest was indicted in 1912 but later acquitted of federal charges of using the mails to defraud by seeking to promote a "worthless device"—the Audion tube.

In 1910 he broadcast a live performance by Enrico Caruso at the Metropolitan Opera in order to popularize the new medium further. In 1912 De Forest conceived the idea of "cascading" a series of Audion tubes so as to amplify high-frequency radio signals far beyond what could be accomplished by merely increasing the voltage on a single tube. He fed the output from the plate of one tube through a transformer to the grid of a second, the output of the second tube's plate to the grid of a third, and so forth, which thereby allowed for an enormous amplification of a signal that was originally very weak. This was an essential development for both radio and telephonic long-distance communication. He also discovered in 1912 that by feeding part of the output of his triode vacuum tube back into its grid, he could cause a self-regenerating oscillation in the circuit. The signal from this circuit, when fed to an antenna system, was far more powerful and effective than that of the crude transmitters then generally employed and, when properly modulated, was capable of transmitting speech and music. When appropriately modified, this single invention was capable of either transmitting, receiving, or amplifying radio signals.

Throughout De Forest's lifetime, the originality of his more important inventions was hotly contested, by both scientists and patent attorneys. In time, realizing that he could not succeed in business or manufacturing, he reluctantly sold his patents to major communications firms for commercial development. Some of the most important of these sales were made at very low prices to the American Telephone & Telegraph Company, which used the Audion as an essential amplification component for long-distance repeater circuits.

Other Inventions

In 1920 De Forest began to work on a practical system for recording and reproducing sound motion pictures. He developed a sound-on-film optical recording system called Phonofilm and demonstrated it in theaters between 1923 and 1927. Although it was basically correct in principle, its operating quality was poor, and he found himself unable to interest film producers in its possibilities. Ironically, within a few years' time the motion-picture industry converted to talking pictures by using a sound-on-film process similar to De Forest's. During the 1930s De Forest developed Audion-diathermy machines for medical applications, and during World War II he conducted military research for Bell Laboratories.

GUGLIELMO MARCONI

(b. April 25, 1874, Bologna, Italy—d. July 20, 1937, Rome)

Italian physicist Guglielmo Marconi was the inventor of a successful wireless telegraph (1896). In 1909 he received the Nobel Prize for Physics, which he shared with German physicist Ferdinand Braun. He later worked on the development of shortwave wireless communication, which constitutes the basis of nearly all modern long-distance radio.

Education and Early Work

Marconi's father was Italian and his mother Irish. Educated first in Bologna and later in Florence, Marconi then went to the technical school in Leghorn, where, in studying physics, he had every opportunity for investigating electromagnetic wave technique, following the earlier mathematical work of James Clerk Maxwell and the experiments of Heinrich Hertz, who first produced and transmitted radio waves, and Sir Oliver Lodge, who conducted research on lightning and electricity.

In 1894 Marconi began experimenting at his father's estate near Bologna, using comparatively crude apparatuses: an induction coil for increasing voltages, with a spark discharger controlled by a Morse key at the sending end and a simple coherer (a device designed to detect radio waves) at the receiver. After preliminary experiments over a short distance, he first improved the coherer; then, by systematic tests, he showed that the range of signaling was increased by using a vertical aerial with a metal plate or cylinder at the top of a pole connected to a similar plate on the ground. The range of signaling was thus increased to about 1.5 miles (2.4 km), enough to convince Marconi of the potentialities of this new system of communication. During this period he also conducted simple experiments with reflectors around the aerial to concentrate the radiated electrical energy into a beam instead of spreading it in all directions.

Receiving little encouragement to continue his experiments in Italy, he went, in 1896, to London, where he was soon assisted by Sir William Preece, the chief engineer of the post office. Marconi filed his first patent in England in June 1896 and, during that and the following year, gave a series of successful demonstrations, in some of which he used balloons and kites to obtain greater height for his aerials. He was able to send signals over distances of up to 4 miles (6.4 km) on the Salisbury Plain and to nearly 9 miles (14.5 km) across the Bristol Channel. These tests, together with Preece's lectures on them, attracted considerable publicity both in England and abroad, and in June 1897 Marconi went to La Spezia, where a land station was erected and communication was established with Italian warships at distances of up to 11.8 miles (19 km).

There remained much skepticism about the useful application of this means of communication and a lack of interest in its exploitation. But Marconi's cousin Jameson Davis, a practicing engineer, financed his patent and helped in the formation of the Wireless Telegraph and Signal Company, Ltd. (changed in 1900 to Marconi's Wireless Telegraph Company, Ltd.). During the first years, the company's efforts were devoted chiefly to showing the full possibilities of radiotelegraphy. A further step was taken in 1899 when a wireless station was established at South Foreland, England, for communicating with Wimereux in France, a distance of 30 miles (50 km); in the same year, British battleships exchanged messages at 75 miles (120 km).

In September 1899 Marconi equipped two American ships to report to newspapers in New York City the progress of the yacht race for the America's Cup. The success of this demonstration aroused worldwide excitement and led to the formation of the American Marconi Company. The following year the Marconi International Marine Communication Company, Ltd., was established for the purpose of installing and operating services between ships and land stations. In 1900 also, Marconi filed his now-famous patent No. 7777 for Improvements in Apparatus for Wireless Telegraphy. The patent, based in part on earlier work in wireless telegraphy by Sir Oliver Lodge, enabled several stations to operate on different wavelengths without interference. (In 1943 the U.S. Supreme Court overturned patent No. 7777, indicating that Lodge, Nikola Tesla, and John Stone appeared to have priority in the development of radio-tuning apparatus.)

Major Discoveries and Innovations

Marconi's great triumph was, however, yet to come. In spite of the opinion expressed by some distinguished mathematicians that the curvature of the earth would limit practical communication by means of electric waves to a distance of 100 to 200 miles (160 to 320 km), Marconi succeeded in December 1901 in receiving at Saint John's, Newfoundland, signals transmitted across the Atlantic Ocean from Poldhu in Cornwall, England. This achievement created an immense sensation in every part of the civilized world, and, though much remained to be learned about the laws of propagation of radio waves around the Earth and through the atmosphere, it was the starting point of the vast development of radio communications, broadcasting, and navigation services that took place in the next 50 years, in much of which Marconi himself continued to play an important part.

Guglielmo Marconi, c. *1908.*

During a voyage on

the U.S. liner *Philadelphia* in 1902, Marconi received messages from distances of 700 miles (1,125 km) by day and 2,000 miles (3,200 km) by night. He thus was the first to discover that, because some radio waves travel by reflection from the upper regions of the atmosphere, transmission conditions are sometimes more favorable at night than during the day. This circumstance is due to the fact that the upward travel of the waves is limited in the daytime by absorption in the lower atmosphere, which becomes ionized—and so electrically conducting—under the influence of sunlight. In 1902 also, Marconi patented the magnetic detector in which the magnetization in a moving band of iron wires is changed by the arrival of a signal causing a click in the telephone receiver connected to it. During the ensuing three years, he also developed and patented the horizontal directional aerial. Both of these devices improved the efficiency of the communication system. In 1910 he received messages at Buenos Aires from Clifden in Ireland over a distance of approximately 6,000 miles (10,000 km), using a wavelength of about 5 miles (8,000 m). Two years later Marconi introduced further innovations that so improved transmission and reception that important long-distance stations could be established. This increased efficiency allowed Marconi to send the first radio message from England to Australia in September 1918.

In spite of the rapid and widespread developments then taking place in radio and its applications to maritime use, Marconi's intuition and urge to experiment were by no means exhausted. In 1916, during World War I, he saw the possible advantages of shorter wavelengths that would permit the use of reflectors around the aerial, thus minimizing the interception of transmitted signals by the enemy and also effecting an increase in signal strength.

After tests in Italy (20 years after his original experiments with reflectors), Marconi continued the work in Great Britain and, on a wavelength of 50 feet (15 m), received signals over a range of 20 to 100 miles (30 to 160 km). In 1923 the experiments were continued on board his steam yacht *Elettra*, which had been specially equipped. From a transmitter of 1 kilowatt at Poldhu, Cornwall, signals were received at a distance of 1,400 miles (2,250 km). These signals were much louder than those from Caernarfon, Wales, on a wavelength several hundred times as great and with 100 times the power at the transmitter. Thus began the development of shortwave wireless communication that, with the use of the beam aerial system for concentrating the energy in the desired direction, is the basis of most modern long-distance radio communication. In 1924 the Marconi company obtained a contract from the post office to establish shortwave communication between England and the countries of the British Commonwealth.

A few years later Marconi returned to the study of still shorter waves of about 20 inches (50 cm). At these very short wavelengths, a parabolic reflector of moderate size gives a considerable increase in power in the desired direction. Experiments conducted off the coast of Italy on the yacht *Elettra* soon showed that useful ranges of communication could be achieved with low-powered transmitters. In 1932, using very short wavelengths, Marconi installed a radiotelephone system between Vatican City and the pope's palace at Castel Gandolfo. In later work Marconi once more demonstrated that even radio waves as short as 22 inches (55 cm) are not limited in range to the horizon or to optical distance between transmitter and receiver.

Marconi received many honors and several honorary degrees. He was awarded the Nobel Prize for Physics (1909) for the development of wireless telegraphy; sent as plenipotentiary delegate to the peace conference in Paris (1919), in which capacity he signed the peace treaties with Austria and with Bulgaria; created marchese and nominated to the Italian senate (1929); and chosen president of the Royal Italian Academy (1930).

ROBERT GODDARD

(b. Oct. 5, 1882, Worcester, Mass., U.S.—d. Aug. 10, 1945, Baltimore, Md.)

Robert Hutchings Goddard was an American professor and inventor generally acknowledged to be the father of modern rocketry. He published his classic treatise, *A Method of Reaching Extreme Altitudes*, in 1919.

Early Life and Training

Goddard was the only child of a bookkeeper, salesman, and machine-shop owner of modest means. The boy had a genteel upbringing and in early youth felt the excitement of the post-Civil War Industrial Revolution when Worcester factories were producing machinery and goods for the burgeoning country. From childhood on he displayed great curiosity about physical phenomena and a bent toward inventiveness. He read in physics and mechanics and dreamed of great inventions.

In 1898 young Goddard's imagination was fired by the H.G. Wells space-fiction novel *War of the Worlds*, then serialized in the *Boston Post*. Shortly thereafter, as he recounted, he actually dreamed of constructing a workable space-flight machine. On October 19, 1899, a day that became his "Anniversary Day," he climbed a cherry tree in his backyard and ". . . imagined how wonderful it would be to make some device which had even the *possibility* of ascending to Mars . . . when I descended the tree . . . ," he wrote in his diary, "existence at last seemed very purposive."

Goddard's fascination with space flight and the means of attaining it continued into his college years at the Worcester Polytechnic Institute. In an assigned theme, "Traveling in 1950," he was also intrigued with the notion of "the fastest possible travel for living bodies on the earth's surface" and projected a plan for travel inside a steel vacuum tube in which cars were suspended and driven by the attraction and repulsion of electromagnets. Patents on a vacuum-tube system of transport were later granted the inventor, with thrust—acceleration and deceleration—the chief principle.

Research in Massachusetts

In 1908 Goddard began a long association with Clark University, Worcester, where he earned his doctorate, taught physics, and carried out rocket experiments. In his small laboratory there, he was the first to prove that thrust and consequent propulsion can take place in a vacuum, needing no air to push against. He was the first to explore mathematically the ratios of energy and thrust per weight of various fuels, including liquid oxygen and liquid hydrogen. He was also the first to develop a rocket motor using liquid fuels (liquid oxygen and gasoline), as used in the German V-2 rocket weapon 15 years later. In a small structure adjoining his laboratory, a liquid-propelled rocket in a static test in 1925 "operated satisfactorily and lifted its own weight," he wrote. On March 16, 1926, the world's first flight of a liquid-propelled rocket engine took place on his Aunt Effie's farm in Auburn, Massachusetts, achieving a brief liftoff.

As is frequently the case with scientific theory and invention, developments proceeded in various parts of the world. In achieving liftoff of his small but sophisticated rocket engine, Goddard carried his experiments further than did the Russian and German space pioneers of the day. While Goddard was engaged in building models of a space-bound vehicle, he was unaware that an obscure schoolteacher in a remote village of Russia was equally fascinated by the potential for space flight. In 1903 Konstantin E. Tsiolkovsky wrote "Investigations of Space by Means of Rockets," which many years later was hailed by the Soviet Union as the forerunner of space flight. The other member of the pioneer space trio—Hermann Oberth of Germany—published his space–flight treatise, *Die Rakete zu den Planetenräumen*, in 1923, four years after the appearance of Goddard's early monograph.

Goddard's early tests and others were modestly financed over a period of several years by the Smithsonian Institution, whose secretary, Charles G. Abbot, had responded to Goddard's appeal for financial support. In 1929, following an aborted and noisy flight test that brought unwanted press notice to the publicity-shy inventor, Charles A. Lindbergh was instrumental in procuring greater financial assistance for Goddard's experiments. From 1930 to the mid-1940s, the Guggenheim Fund for the Promotion of Aeronautics financed the work on a scale that made possible a small shop and crew and experimental flights in the open spaces of the American southwest, at Roswell, New Mexico. There, Goddard spent most of his remaining days in the unending trial-and-error reach for high altitudes.

Experiments at Roswell

In the course of his experiments there he became the first to shoot a liquid-fuel rocket faster than the speed of sound (1935). He obtained the first patents of a steering apparatus for the rocket machine and of the use of "step rockets" to gain great altitudes. He also developed the first pumps suitable for rocket fuels, self-cooling rocket motors, and other components of an engine designed to carry man to outer space. Furthermore, his experiments and calculations took place at a time when any news of his work drew from the press and the public high amusement that "Moony" Goddard could take seriously the possibility of travel beyond Earth. His small rockets, early prototypes of the modern Moon thrusters, achieved altitudes of up to 1 mile (1.6 km) above the prairie.

During World War II, Goddard offered his work to the military, but lack of interest in rocket development led to his closing down the Roswell establishment and participating in the war effort through a small Navy contract for work at Annapolis, Maryland, on the development of a jet-thrust booster for seaplane takeoff. Lindbergh and the industrialist and philanthropist Harry F. Guggenheim remained staunch advocates of the Worcester inventor and the feasibility of space exploration.

Goddard died of throat cancer in 1945, at the threshold of the age of jet and rocket. Years later, his work was acknowledged by the United States government when a $1,000,000 settlement was made for the use of his patents. The Goddard Memorial Library at Clark University was named in his honor.

CLARENCE BIRDSEYE

(b. Dec. 9, 1886, New York, N.Y., U.S.—d. Oct. 7, 1956, New York)

Clarence Birdseye was an American businessman and inventor best known for developing a process for freezing foods in small packages suitable for retailing.

After working as a government naturalist, Birdseye went to Labrador as a fur trader in 1912 and again in 1916.

There the people often froze food in the winter because of the difficulty of obtaining fresh food; this solution to their problem spurred Birdseye's imagination.

After returning to the United States, he began to experiment. In 1924 he helped found General Seafoods Company, having developed two processes for freezing fish based on a theory of quick freezing. His first patent, describing a method for preserving piscatorial products, involved placing food between two metal plates that were chilled by a calcium chloride solution to approximately -40 °F (-40 °C). The second process utilized two hollow metal plates that were cooled to -13 °F (-25 °C) by vaporization of ammonia. In 1929 Birdseye began selling his quick-frozen foods, a successful line of products that made him wealthy. Though his were not the first frozen foods, Birdseye's freezing processes were highly efficient ones that preserved the original flavor of a variety of foods, including fish, fruits, and vegetables. In 1929 Birdseye's company was bought by Postum, Inc., which changed its own name to the General Foods Corporation, retaining Birdseye as a consultant. From 1930 to 1934 Birdseye was president of Birds Eye Frosted Foods and from 1935 to 1938, of Birdseye Electric Company.

Birdseye held nearly 300 patents. Besides his frozen food process, he developed infrared heat lamps, a recoilless harpoon gun for taking whales, and a method of removing water from foods. A few years before his death he perfected a method of converting bagasse (crushed sugarcane residue) into paper pulp.

IGOR SIKORSKY

(b. May 25, 1889, Kiev, Russia—d. Oct. 26, 1972, Easton, Conn., U.S.)

Igor Ivan Sikorsky was a Russian-born U.S. pioneer in aircraft design who is best known for his successful development of the helicopter.

Education and Early Career

Sikorsky's father was a physician and professor of psychology. His mother also was a physician but never practiced professionally. Her great interest in art and in the life and work of Leonardo da Vinci undoubtedly stimulated her son's early interest in experimenting with model flying machines; when he was 12 years old he made a small rubber-powered helicopter that could rise in the air.

In 1903 Sikorsky entered the Naval Academy in Saint Petersburg, with the intention of becoming a career officer, but his interest in engineering led to his resignation from the service in 1906. After a brief period of engineering study in Paris, he entered the Kiev Polytechnic Institute. Following a reasonably successful academic year, however, he concluded that the abstract sciences and the higher mathematics as then taught had little relationship to the solution of practical problems, and he left the school, preferring to spend his time in his own shop and laboratory.

A trip through Europe in the summer of 1908 brought him into contact with the accomplishments of the Wright brothers and the group of European inventors who were trying to match their progress in flight. Returning to Kiev, Sikorsky came to the conclusion that the way to fly was "straight up," as Leonardo had proposed, a concept that called for a horizontal rotor. Assisted financially by his sister Olga, he returned to Paris in January 1909 for further study and to purchase a lightweight engine.

Back in Kiev in May of 1909 he began construction of a helicopter. Its failure revealed some of the practical obstacles. A second machine with a larger engine was tested in 1910, but it also failed to fly. He then made a major decision: "I had learned enough to recognize that with the existing state of the art, engines, materials, and—most of all—the shortage of money and lack of experience . . . I would not be able to produce a successful helicopter at that time." In fact, he had to wait 30 years before all conditions could be met.

For the time being Sikorsky decided to enter the field of fixed-wing design and began construction of his first airplane. Sikorsky's S-1 biplane was tested early in 1910, and, although its 15-horsepower engine proved inadequate, a redesigned airframe with a larger engine (S-2) carried him on his first short flight. The S-3, S-4, and S-5 followed in quick succession, each a refinement of its predecessor, and each adding to his piloting experience. Finally, by the summer of 1911, in an S-5 with a 50-horsepower engine, he was able to remain in the air for more than an hour, attain altitudes of 1,500 feet (450 m), and make short cross-country flights. This success earned him International Pilot's License Number 64.

The subsequent S-6 series established Sikorsky as a serious competitor for supplying aircraft to the Russian Army. Characteristically, he soon took a giant step: the first four-engined airplane, called "Le Grand," the precursor of many modern bombers and commercial transports, which he built and flew successfully by 1913. Among its innovative features, not adopted elsewhere until the middle 1920s, was a completely enclosed cabin for pilots and passengers.

In the period of disruption following the Russian Revolution and the collapse of Germany, Sikorsky saw little opportunity for further aircraft development in Europe. He decided to start over again in the United States and in March 1919 landed in New York as an immigrant.

Work in the United States

After several lean years as a lecturer and schoolteacher, while trying to find a place for himself in the contracting postwar aircraft industry, he and a few associates, some of them former Russian officers, formed their own company, the Sikorsky Aero Engineering Corporation. They set up shop in an old barn on a farm near Roosevelt Field on Long Island. Sikorsky became a U.S. citizen in 1928. By 1929 the company, having become a division of United Aircraft Corporation, occupied a large modern plant at Bridgeport, Connecticut, and was producing S-38 twin-engined amphibians in considerable numbers. In 1931 the first S-40, the "American Clipper," pioneered Pan American World Airways mail and passenger routes around the Caribbean and to South America. By the summer of 1937 Pan American began transpacific and transatlantic service with the first four-engined S-42 "Clipper," the last of the Sikorsky series, the ancestor of which had been "Le Grand" of 1913.

By the late 1930s changing requirements for military and commercial air transport forecast the termination of the large flying boat, and Sikorsky returned to his first love, the helicopter. Once again he was involved in "advanced pioneering work . . . where extremely little reliable information and no piloting experience whatever were available." The essential aerodynamic theory and construction techniques that had been lacking in 1910, however, were now available. Early in 1939, with a well-trained engineering group at his disposal, he started the construction of the VS-300 helicopter. As he said later, "There was a great satisfaction in knowing that, within a short period of time, good engineering along a novel line produced encouraging results." On September 14, 1939, the VS-300 lifted off the ground on its first flight. Its designer was at the controls; during his entire career Sikorsky always insisted on making the first trial flight of any new design himself. On May 6, 1941, in an improved machine, he established an international endurance record of one hour 32.4 seconds.

It is doubtful that Sikorsky at that time fully envisioned the remarkable development of the vertical-lift machine in the next 30 years. Certainly he did not anticipate widespread use of the helicopter as an offensive military weapon. He regarded it as a useful tool for industry and air commerce but primarily as an effective device for rescue and relief of human beings caught in natural disasters, such as fire, flood, or famine. He estimated that more than 50,000 lives had been saved by helicopters.

Igor Sikorsky's active professional life covered virtually the entire span of practical flight by man, from the Wright brothers to space exploration. Few in aviation can claim such a span of personal participation, or personal contribution with such a wide range of innovative ideas. He only complained that, of all his past predictions, those that he lived to regret were on the "too conservative" side.

Sikorsky retired as engineering manager for his company in 1957 but remained active as a consultant until his death. In addition to his wife (married in 1924), he left one daughter and four sons. Sikorsky received many honorary doctorates in science and engineering, honorary fellowships in leading scientific and technical societies in the United States and Europe, and the highest medals and awards in aviation, including the Cross of St. Vladimir from Russia; the Sylvanus Albert Reed Award for 1942 from the Institute of Aeronautical Sciences in New York; the United States Presidential Certificate of Merit in 1948; the Daniel Guggenheim Medal and Certificate for

1951; the Elmer A. Sperry Award for 1964; and the National Defense Award in 1971.

Sikorsky's *Recollections and Thoughts of a Pioneer* (1964) reviews his own career and accomplishments and includes his views on the future trends of aviation development. *The Story of the Winged-S: Late Developments and Recent Photographs of the Helicopter*, rev. ed. (1967), an autobiography, includes a detailed account of his life and work through 1938, with supplementary chapters on his first helicopter experiments of 1939–40 and later work.

VLADIMIR ZWORYKIN

(b. July 30, 1889, Murom, Russia—d. July 29, 1982, Princeton, N.J., U.S.)

Vladimir Kosma Zworykin, a Russian-born American electronic engineer and inventor, is considered to be the father of modern television.

After education at the Saint Petersburg Institute of Technology and the Collegè de France, in Paris, Zworykin served during World War I in the Russian Signal Corps. He emigrated to the United States in 1919 and became a naturalized citizen in 1924. In 1920 he joined the Westinghouse Electric Corporation in Pittsburgh, and in 1923 he filed a patent application for an all-electronic television system, although he was as yet unable to build and demonstrate it. In 1929 he convinced David Sarnoff, vice president and general manager of Westinghouse's parent company, the Radio Corporation of America (RCA), to support his research by predicting that in two years, with $100,000 of funding, he could produce a workable electronic television system. Meanwhile, the first demonstration of a primitive electronic system had been made in San Francisco in 1927 by Philo Taylor

Farnsworth, a young man with only a high-school education. Farnsworth had garnered research funds by convincing his investors that he could market an economically viable television system in six months for an investment of only $5,000. In the event, it took the efforts of both men and more than $50 million before anyone made a profit.

With his first $100,000 of RCA research money, Zworykin developed a workable cathode-ray receiver that he called the Kinescope. At the same time, Farnsworth was perfecting his Image Dissector camera tube. In 1930 Zworykin visited Farnsworth's laboratory and was given a demonstration of the Image Dissector. At that point a healthy cooperation might have arisen between the two pioneers, but competition, spurred by the vision of corporate profits, kept them apart. Sarnoff offered Farnsworth $100,000 for his patents but was summarily turned down. Farnsworth instead accepted an offer to join RCA's rival Philco, but he soon left to set up his own firm. Then in 1931 Zworykin's RCA team, after learning much from the study of Farnsworth's Image Dissector, came up with the Iconoscope camera tube, and with it they finally had a working electronic system.

Zworykin's television system provided the impetus for the development of modern television as an entertainment and education medium. Although ultimately replaced by the orthicon and image orthicon tubes, the Iconoscope was the basis for further important developments in television cameras. The modern television picture tube is basically Zworykin's Kinescope. He also developed a color-television system, for which he received a patent in 1928. His other developments in electronics include an early form of the electric eye and innovations in the electron microscope. His electron image tube, sensitive to infrared light, was the basis for the sniperscope and the snooperscope, devices first used in World War II for seeing in the dark. His secondary-emission multiplier was used in the scintillation counter, one of the most sensitive of radiation detectors.

In later life Zworykin lamented the way television had been abused to titillate and trivialize subjects rather than for the educational and cultural enrichment of audiences.

Named an honorary vice president of RCA in 1954, from then until 1962 Zworykin also served as director of the medical electronics center of the Rockefeller Institute for Medical Research (now Rockefeller University) in New York City. In 1967 the National Academy of Sciences awarded him the National Medal of Science for his contributions to the instruments of science, engineering, and television and for his stimulation of the application of engineering to medicine. He was also founder-president of the International Federation for Medical Electronics and Biological Engineering, a recipient of the Faraday Medal from Great Britain (1965) and the U.S. Presidential Medal of Science (1966), and a member of the U.S. National Hall of Fame from 1977.

Zworykin wrote *Photocells and Their Applications* (1932), *Television* (1940; rev. ed., 1954), *Electron Optics and the Electron Microscope* (1946), *Photoelectricity and Its Application* (1949), and *Television in Science and Industry* (1958).

EDWIN H. ARMSTRONG

(b. Dec. 18, 1890, New York, N.Y., U.S.—d. Jan. 31/Feb. 1, 1954, New York City)

American inventor Edwin Howard Armstrong laid the foundation for much of modern radio and electronic circuitry, including the regenerative and superheterodyne circuits and the frequency modulation (FM) system.

Early Life

Armstrong was from a genteel, devoutly Presbyterian family of Manhattan. His father was a publisher and his mother a former schoolteacher. Armstrong was a shy boy interested from childhood in engines, railway trains, and all mechanical contraptions.

At age 14, fired by reading of the exploits of Guglielmo Marconi in sending the first wireless message across the Atlantic Ocean, Armstrong decided to become an inventor. He built a maze of wireless apparatus in his family's attic and began the solitary, secretive work that absorbed his life. Except for a passion for tennis and, later, for fast motor cars, he developed no other significant interests. Wireless was then in the stage of crude spark-gap transmitters and iron-filing receivers, producing faint Morse-code signals, barely audible through tight earphones. Armstrong joined in the hunt for improved instruments. On graduating from high school, he commuted to Columbia University's School of Engineering.

In his junior year at Columbia, Armstrong made his first, most seminal invention. Among the devices investigated for better wireless reception was the then little understood, largely unused Audion, or three-element vacuum tube, invented in 1906 by Lee De Forest, a pioneer in the development of wireless telegraphy and television. Armstrong made exhaustive measurements to find out how the tube worked and devised a circuit, called the regenerative, or feedback, circuit, that suddenly, in the autumn of 1912, brought in signals with a thousandfold amplification, loud enough to be heard across a room. At its highest amplification, the tube's circuit shifted from being a receiver to being an oscillator, or primary generator, of wireless waves. As a radio wave generator, this circuit is still at the heart of all radio and television broadcasting.

Armstrong's priority was later challenged by De Forest in a monumental series of corporate patent suits, extending more than 14 years, argued twice before the U.S. Supreme Court, and finally ending—in a judicial misunderstanding of the nature of the invention—in favor of De Forest. But the scientific community never accepted this verdict. The Institute of Radio Engineers refused to revoke an earlier gold-medal award to Armstrong for the discovery of the feedback circuit. Later he received the Franklin Medal, highest of the United States' scientific honors, reaffirming his invention of the regenerative circuit.

This youthful invention that opened the age of electronics had profound effects on Armstrong's life. It led him, after a stint as an instructor at Columbia University, into the U.S. Army Signal Corps laboratories in World War I in Paris, where he invented the superheterodyne circuit, a highly selective means of receiving, converting, and greatly amplifying very weak, high-frequency electromagnetic waves, which today underlies 98 percent of all radio, radar, and television reception over the airways. It brought him into early association with the man destined to lead the postwar Radio Corporation of America (RCA), David Sarnoff, whose young secretary Armstrong later married. Armstrong himself returned after the war to Columbia University to become assistant to Michael Pupin, the notable physicist and inventor and his revered teacher. In this period he sold patent rights on his circuits to the major corporations, including RCA, for large sums in cash and stock. Suddenly, in the radio boom of the 1920s, he found himself a millionaire. But he continued to teach at Columbia, financing his own research, working along with Pupin, whose professorship he inherited, on the long-unsolved problem of eliminating static from radio.

Invention of FM Broadcasting

In 1933 Armstrong secured four patents on advanced circuits that were to solve this last basic problem. They revealed an entirely new radio system, from transmitter to receiver. Instead of varying the amplitude, or power, of radio waves to carry voice or music, as in all radio before then, the new system varied, or modulated, the waves' frequency (number of waves per second) over a wide band of frequencies. This created a carrier wave that natural static—an amplitude phenomenon created by electrical storms—could not break into. As a result, FM's wide frequency range made possible the first clear, practical method of high-fidelity broadcasting.

Because the new system required a basic change in transmitters and receivers, it was not embraced with any alacrity by the established radio industry. Armstrong had to build the first full-scale FM station himself in 1939 at a cost of more than $300,000 to prove its worth. He then had to develop and promote the system, sustain it through World War II (while he again turned to military research), and fight off postwar regulatory attempts to hobble FM's growth. When FM slowly established itself, Armstrong again found himself entrapped in another interminable patent suit to retain his invention. Ill and aging in 1954, with most of his wealth gone in the battle for FM, he took his own life.

The years have brought increasing recognition of Armstrong's place in science and invention. FM is now the preferred system in radio, the required sound channel in all television, and the dominant medium in mobile radio, microwave relay, and space-satellite communications. Posthumously, Armstrong was elected to the pantheon of electrical greats by the International Telecommunications

Union, to join such figures as André-Marie Ampère, Alexander Graham Bell, Michael Faraday, and Guglielmo Marconi.

R. BUCKMINSTER FULLER

(b. July 12, 1895, Milton, Mass., U.S.—d. July 1, 1983, Los Angeles, Calif.)

Richard Buckminster Fuller was a U.S. engineer and architect who developed the geodesic dome, the only large dome that can be set directly on the ground as a complete structure, and the only practical kind of building that has no limiting dimensions (i.e., beyond which the structural strength must be insufficient). Among the most noteworthy geodesic domes is the United States pavilion for Expo 67 in Montreal. Also a poet and a philosopher, he was noted for unorthodox ideas on global issues.

Life

Fuller was descended from a long line of New England Nonconformists, the most famous of whom was his great-aunt, Margaret Fuller, the critic, teacher, woman of letters and cofounder of *The Dial*, organ of the Transcendentalist movement. Fuller was twice expelled from Harvard University and never completed his formal education. He saw service in the U.S. Navy during World War I as commander of a crash-boat flotilla. In 1917 he married Anne Hewlett, daughter of James Monroe Hewlett, a well-known architect and muralist. Hewlett had invented a modular construction system using a compressed fiber block, and after the war Fuller and Hewlett formed a construction company that used this material (later known as Soundex, a Celotex product) in modules for house construction. In this operation Fuller himself supervised the erection of several hundred houses.

The construction company encountered financial difficulties in 1927, and Fuller, a minority stockholder, was forced out. He found himself stranded in Chicago, without income, alienated, dismayed, confused. At this point in his life, Fuller resolved to devote his remaining years to a nonprofit search for design patterns that could maximize the social uses of the world's energy resources and evolving industrial complex. The inventions, discoveries, and economic strategies that followed were interim factors related to that end.

In 1927, in the course of the development of his comprehensive strategy, he invented and demonstrated a factory-assembled, air-deliverable house, later called the Dymaxion house, which had its own utilities. He designed in 1928, and manufactured in 1933, the first prototype of his three-wheeled omnidirectional vehicle, the Dymaxion car. This automobile, the first streamlined car, could cross open fields like a jeep, accelerate to 120 miles (190 km) per hour, make a 180-degree turn in its own length, carry 12 passengers, and average 28 miles per gallon (12 km per liter) of gasoline. In 1943, at the request of the industrialist Henry Kaiser, Fuller developed a new version of the Dymaxion car that was planned to be powered by three separate air-cooled engines, each coupled to its own wheel by a variable fluid drive. The projected 1943 Dymaxion, like its predecessor, was never commercially produced.

Assuming that there is in nature a vectorial, or directionally oriented, system of forces that provides maximum strength with minimum structures, as is the case in the nested tetrahedron lattices of organic compounds and of metals, Fuller developed a vectorial system of geometry that he called "Energetic-Synergetic geometry." The basic unit of this system is the tetrahedron (a pyramid shape with four sides, including the base), which, in combination with octahedrons (eight-sided shapes), forms the most economic space-filling structures. The architectural consequence of the use of this geometry by Fuller was the geodesic dome, a frame the total strength of which increases in logarithmic ratio to its size. Many thousands of geodesic domes have been erected in various parts of the world, the most publicized of which was the U.S. exhibition dome at Expo 67 in Montreal. One houses the tropical exhibit area of a Saint Louis botanical garden; another, the Union Tank Car Company's dome, was built in 1958 in Baton Rouge, Louisiana, and was demolished in 2007. This dome, at the time of its construction the largest clear-span structure in existence, was 384 feet (117 m) in diameter and 116 feet (35 m) in height.

Other inventions and developments by Fuller included a system of cartography that presents all the land areas of the world without significant distortion; die-stamped prefabricated bathrooms; tetrahedronal floating cities; underwater geodesic-domed farms; and expendable paper domes. Fuller did not regard himself as an inventor or an architect, however. All of his developments, in his view, were accidental or interim incidents in a strategy that aimed at a radical solution of world problems by finding the means to do more with less.

Comprehensive and anticipatory design initiative alone, he held—exclusive of politics and political theory—can solve the problems of human shelter, nutrition, transportation, and pollution; and it can solve these with a fraction of the materials now inefficiently used. Moreover, energy, ever more available, directed by cumulative information stored in computers, is capable of synthesizing raw materials, of machining and packaging commodities, and of supplying the physical needs of the total global population.

Fuller was a research professor at Southern Illinois University (Carbondale) from 1959 to 1968. In 1968 he was named university professor, in 1972 distinguished university professor, and in 1975 university professor emeritus. Queen Elizabeth II awarded Fuller the Royal Gold Medal for Architecture. He also received the 1968 Gold Medal Award of the National Institute of Arts and Letters.

Assessment

Fuller—architect, engineer, inventor, philosopher, author, cartographer, geometrician, futurist, teacher, and poet—established a reputation as one of the most original thinkers of the second half of the 20th century. He conceived of man as a passenger in a cosmic spaceship—a passenger whose only wealth consists in energy and information. Energy has two phases—associative (as atomic and molecule structures) and dissociative (as radiation)—and, according to the first law of thermodynamics, the energy of the universe cannot be decreased. Information, on the other hand, is negatively entropic; as knowledge, technology, "know-how," it constantly increases. Research engenders research, and each technological advance multiplies the productive wealth of the world community. Consequently, "Spaceship Earth" is a regenerative system whose energy is progressively turned to human advantage and whose wealth increases by geometric increments.

Fuller's book *Nine Chains to the Moon* (1938) is an outline of his general technological strategy for maximizing the social applications of energy resources. He further developed this and other themes in such works as *No More Secondhand God* (1962), *Utopia or Oblivion* (1969), *Operating Manual for Spaceship Earth* (1969), *Earth, Inc.* (1973), and *Critical Path* (1981).

PAUL MÜLLER

(b. Jan. 12, 1899, Olten, Switz.—d. Oct. 12, 1965, Basel)

Paul Hermann Müller was a Swiss chemist who received the Nobel Prize for Physiology or Medicine in 1948 for discovering the potent toxic effects on insects of DDT. With its chemical derivatives, DDT became the most widely used insecticide for more than 20 years and was a major factor in increased world food production and the suppression of insect-borne diseases.

A research chemist at the J.R. Geigy Company, Basel (1925–65), Müller began his career with investigations of dyes and tanning agents. In 1935 he began his search for an "ideal" insecticide, one that would show rapid, potent toxicity for the greatest number of insect species but would cause little or no damage to plants and warm-blooded animals. He also required that it have a high degree of chemical stability, so that its effect would persist for long periods of time and its manufacture would be economical. Four years later Müller tested a substance known as dichlorodiphenyltrichloroethane (DDT) and found that it satisfied these requirements. The German chemist Othmar Zeidler had first synthesized the compound in 1874 but had failed to realize its value as an insecticide.

In 1939 DDT was tested successfully against the Colorado potato beetle by the Swiss government and by the U.S. Department of Agriculture in 1943. In January 1944 DDT was used to quash an outbreak of typhus carried by lice in Naples, the first time a winter typhus epidemic had been stopped.

Although Müller had required his ideal insecticide to be relatively nontoxic to warm-blooded animals, the widespread use and persistence of DDT (in 1968 it was estimated that 1,000,000,000 pounds [453,000,000 kg] of the substance remained in the environment) made it a hazard to animal life, and it showed signs of disrupting ecological food chains. By 1970 DDT was rapidly being supplanted by more quickly degraded, less toxic agents; its use was banned in a number of countries.

ERNEST O. LAWRENCE

(b. Aug. 8, 1901, Canton, S.D., U.S.—d. Aug. 27, 1958, Palo Alto, Calif.)

Ernest Orlando Lawrence, an American physicist, was awarded the 1939 Nobel Prize for Physics for his invention of the cyclotron, the first particle accelerator to achieve high energies.

Lawrence earned his Ph.D. at Yale University in 1925. An assistant professor of physics at Yale (1927–28), he went to the University of California, Berkeley, as an associate professor and became full professor there in 1930.

Lawrence first conceived the idea for the cyclotron in 1929. One of his students, M. Stanley Livingston, undertook the project and succeeded in building a device that accelerated hydrogen ions (protons) to an energy of 13,000 electron volts (eV). Lawrence then set out to build a second cyclotron; when completed, it accelerated protons to 1,200,000 eV, enough energy to cause nuclear disintegration. To continue the program, Lawrence built the Radiation Laboratory at Berkeley in 1936 and was made its director.

One of Lawrence's cyclotrons produced technetium, the first element that does not occur in nature to be made artificially. His basic design was utilized in developing other particle accelerators, which have been largely responsible for the great advances made in the field of particle physics. With the cyclotron, he produced radioactive phosphorus and other isotopes for medical use, including radioactive iodine for the first therapeutic treatment of hyperthyroidism. In addition, he instituted the use of neutron beams in treating cancer.

During World War II he worked with the Manhattan Project as a program chief in charge of the development of the electromagnetic process of separating uranium-235 for the atomic bomb. In 1957 he received the Fermi Award from the U.S. Atomic Energy Commission. Besides his work in nuclear physics, Lawrence invented and patented a color-television picture tube. In his honor were named Lawrence Berkeley Laboratory at Berkeley; Lawrence Livermore National Laboratory at Livermore, California; and element 103, lawrencium.

WALT DISNEY

(b. December 5, 1901, Chicago, Ill., U.S.—d. December 15, 1966, Los Angeles, Calif.),

Walter Elias Disney, an American motion-picture and television producer and showman, became famous as a pioneer of animated cartoon films and as the creator of such cartoon characters as Mickey Mouse and Donald Duck. He also planned and built Disneyland, a huge amusement park that opened near Los Angeles in 1955, and before his death he had begun building a second such park, Walt Disney World, near Orlando, Florida. The Disney Company he founded has become one of the world's largest entertainment conglomerates.

EARLY LIFE

Walt Disney was the fourth son of Elias Disney, a peripatetic carpenter, farmer, and building contractor, and his wife, Flora Call, who had been a public school teacher. When Walt was little more than an infant, the family moved to a farm near Marceline, Missouri, a typical small Midwestern town, which is said to have furnished the inspiration and model for the Main Street, U.S.A., of Disneyland. There Walt began his schooling and first showed a taste and aptitude for drawing and painting with crayons and watercolors.

His restless father soon abandoned his efforts at farming and moved the family to Kansas City, Missouri, where he bought a morning newspaper route and compelled his young sons to assist him in delivering papers. Walt later said that many of the habits and compulsions of his adult life stemmed from the disciplines and discomforts of helping his father with the paper route. In Kansas City the young Walt began to study cartooning with a correspondence school and later took classes at the Kansas City Art Institute and School of Design.

In 1917 the Disneys moved back to Chicago, and Walt entered McKinley High School, where he took photographs, made drawings for the school paper, and studied cartooning on the side, for he was hopeful of eventually achieving a job as a newspaper cartoonist. His progress was interrupted by World War I, in which he participated as an ambulance driver for the American Red Cross in France and Germany.

Returning to Kansas City in 1919, he found

occasional employment as a draftsman and inker in commercial art studios, where he met Ub Iwerks, a young artist whose talents contributed greatly to Walt's early success.

First Animated Cartoons

Dissatisfied with their progress, Disney and Iwerks started a small studio of their own in 1922 and acquired a secondhand movie camera with which they made one and two-minute animated advertising films for distribution to local movie theaters. They also did a series of animated cartoon sketches called *Laugh-O-grams* and the pilot film for a series of seven-minute fairy tales that combined both live action and animation, *Alice in Cartoonland*. A New York film distributor cheated the young producers, and Disney was forced to file for bankruptcy in 1923. He moved to California to pursue a career as a cinematographer, but the surprise success of the first *Alice* film compelled Disney and his brother Roy—a lifelong business partner—to reopen shop in Hollywood.

With Roy as business manager, Disney resumed the *Alice* series, persuading Iwerks to join him and assist with the drawing of the cartoons. They invented a character called Oswald the Lucky Rabbit, contracted for distribution of the films at $1,500 each, and propitiously launched their small enterprise. In 1927, just before the transition to sound in motion pictures, Disney and Iwerks experimented with a new character—a cheerful, energetic, and mischievous mouse called Mickey. They had planned two shorts, called *Plane Crazy* and *Gallopin' Gaucho*, that were to introduce Mickey Mouse when *The Jazz Singer*, a motion picture with the popular singer Al Jolson, brought the novelty of sound to the movies. Fully recognizing the possibilities for sound in animated-cartoon films, Disney quickly produced a third Mickey Mouse cartoon equipped with voices and music, entitled *Steamboat Willie*, and cast aside the other two soundless cartoon films. When it appeared in 1928, *Steamboat Willie* was a sensation.

The following year Disney started a new series called Silly Symphonies with a picture entitled *The Skeleton Dance*, in which a skeleton rises from the graveyard and does a clattering dance set to music based on classical themes. Original and briskly syncopated, the film ensured popular acclaim for the series, but, with costs mounting because of the more complicated drawing and technical work, Disney's operation was continually in peril.

The growing popularity of Mickey Mouse and his girlfriend, Minnie, however, attested to the public's taste for the fantasy of little creatures with the speech, skills, and personality traits of human beings. (Disney himself provided the voice for Mickey until 1947.) This popularity led to the invention of other animal characters, such as Donald Duck and the dogs Pluto and Goofy. In 1933 Disney produced a short, *The Three Little Pigs*, which arrived in the midst of the Great Depression and took the country by storm. Its treatment of the fairy tale of the little pig who works hard and builds his house of brick against the huffing and puffing of a threatening wolf suited the need for fortitude in the face of economic disaster, and its song *Who's Afraid of the Big Bad Wolf?* was a happy taunting of adversity. It was in this period of economic hard times in the early 1930s that Disney fully endeared himself and his cartoons to audiences all over the world, and his operation began making money in spite of the Depression.

Disney had by that time gathered a staff of creative young people, who were headed by Iwerks. Color was introduced in the Academy Award-winning Silly Symphonies film *Flowers and Trees* (1932), while other animal characters came and went in films such as *The Grasshopper and the Ants* (1934) and *The Tortoise and the Hare* (1935). Roy franchised tie-in sales with the cartoons of Mickey Mouse and Donald Duck—watches, dolls, shirts, and tops—and reaped more wealth for the company.

Feature-length Cartoons

Walt Disney was never one to rest or stand still. He had long thought of producing feature-length animated films in addition to the shorts. In 1934 he began work on a version of the classic fairy tale *Snow White and the Seven Dwarfs* (1937), a project that required great organization and coordination of studio talent and a task for which Disney possessed a unique capacity. While he actively engaged in all phases of creation in his films, he functioned chiefly as coordinator and final decision maker rather than as designer and artist. *Snow White* was widely acclaimed by critics and audiences alike as an amusing and sentimental romance. By animating substantially human figures in the characters of Snow White, the Prince, and the Wicked Queen and by forming caricatures of human figures in the seven dwarfs, Disney departed from the scope and techniques of the shorts and thus proved animation's effectiveness as a vehicle for feature-length stories.

While Disney continued to do short films presenting the anthropomorphic characters of his little animals, he was henceforth to develop a wide variety of full-length entertainment films, such as *Pinocchio* (1940), *Dumbo* (1941), and *Bambi* (1942). Disney also produced a totally unusual and exciting film—his multisegmented and stylized *Fantasia* (1940), in which cartoon figures and color patterns were animated to the music of Igor Stravinsky, Paul Dukas, Pyotr Ilyich Tchaikovsky, and others. In 1940 Disney moved his company into a new studio in Burbank, California, abandoning the old plant it had occupied in the early days of growth.

Major Films and Television Productions

A strike by Disney animators in 1941 was a major setback for the company. Many top animators resigned, and it would be many years before the company produced animated features that lived up to the quality of its early 1940s classics. Disney's foray into films for the federal government during World War II helped the studio perfect methods of combining live-action and animation; the studio's commercial films using this hybrid technique include *The Reluctant Dragon* (1941), *Saludos Amigos* (1942), *The Three Caballeros* (1945), *Make Mine Music* (1946), and *Song of the South* (1946).

The Disney studio by that time was established as a big-business enterprise and began to produce a variety of entertainment films. One popular series, called *True-Life Adventures*, featured nature-based motion pictures such as *Seal Island* (1948), *Beaver Valley* (1950), and *The Living Desert* (1953). The Disney studio also began making full-length animation romances, such as *Cinderella* (1950), *Alice in Wonderland* (1951), and *Peter Pan* (1953), and produced low-budget, live-action films, including *The Absent-Minded Professor* (1961).

The Disney studio was among the first to foresee the potential of television as a popular-entertainment medium and to produce films directly for it. The *Zorro* and *Davy Crockett* series were very popular with children, and *Walt Disney's Wonderful World of Color* became a Sunday-night fixture. But the climax of Disney's career as a theatrical film producer came with his release in 1964 of the motion picture *Mary Poppins*, which won worldwide popularity.

Disneyland

In the early 1950s Disney had initiated plans for a huge amusement park to be built near Los Angeles. When Disneyland opened in 1955, much of Disney's disposition toward nostalgic sentiment and fantasy was evident in its design and construction. It soon became a mecca for tourists from around the world. A second Disney park, Walt Disney World, near Orlando, Florida, was under construction at the time of his death. It opened in 1971.

Assessment

Disney's imagination and energy, his whimsical humor, and his gift for being attuned to the vagaries of popular taste inspired him to develop well-loved amusements for "children of all ages" throughout the world. Although some criticized his frequently saccharine subject matter and accused him of creating a virtual stylistic monopoly in American animation that discouraged experimentation, there is no denying his pathbreaking accomplishments. His achievement as a creator of entertainment for an almost unlimited public and as a highly ingenious merchandiser of his wares can rightly be compared to the most successful industrialists in history.

GLOSSARY

adversity: A difficult situation or hardship.

aeronautics: The science of flight and airplanes.

chassis: The frame, wheels, and machinery of a motor vehicle.

insolvent: Unable to pay debts.

mountebank: A dishonest or cheating person.

oscillation: The act of regularly moving from one position to another and back.

patent: Rights given to a person by the government to make, use, or sell an invention.

prototype: An original model on which something is based.

subsistence: The amount of material goods needed to survive.

syncopated: Having a rhythm that stresses the weak beats instead of the strong beats.

transistor: An electronic device that can transform weak electrical signals into strong ones, acting as an amplifier.

treatise: A formal exposition in writing, generally longer and more specific than an essay.

For More Information

BOOKS

Calvert, Jennifer. *Teen Trailblazers: 30 Daring Boys Whose Dreams Changed the World.* New York, NY: Castle Point Books, 2022.

Kirkfield, Vivian. *From Here to There: Inventions That Changed the Way the World Moves*. Boston, MA: Houghton Mifflin Harcourt, 2021.

Murray, Julie. *Automobile.* Minneapolis, MN: ABDO, 2023.

Rubio, Elizabeth. *Understanding and Using Radio Waves.* New York, NY: Enslow Publishing, 2022

WEBSITES

Henry Ford Museum
www.thehenryford.org/
The Henry Ford Museum celebrates Ford's legacy and preserves pieces of the past.

Igor Sikorsky Historical Archives
sikorskyarchives.com/home/igor-sikorsky/
View photos of Igor Sikorsky and his inventions on this website.

National Air and Space Museum: The Wright Brothers
airandspace.si.edu/explore/stories/wright-brothers
This website provides images, explanations, and historical context for the great achievements of the Wright Brothers.

The Walt Disney Family Museum
www.waltdisney.org/
You can learn more about Walt Disney's life at this museum dedicated to his art and impact on the world.

Index